The Big Bird Spot

A globe-trotting bird-spotting adventure

Matt Sewell

PAVILION

For Romy and Mae

First published in the United Kingdom in 2017 by
Pavilion Children's Books
43 Great Ormond Street
London
WC1N 3HZ

An imprint of Pavilion Books Limited.

Publisher and Editor: Neil Dunnicliffe
Art Director: Lee-May Lim

ISBN: 9781843653264

A CIP catalogue record for this book is available from the British Library.

10 9 8 7 6 5 4 3 2 1

Reproduction by Mission, Hong Kong
Printed by G. Canale & C., Italy

This book can be ordered directly from the publisher online
at www.pavilionbooks.com, or try your local bookshop.

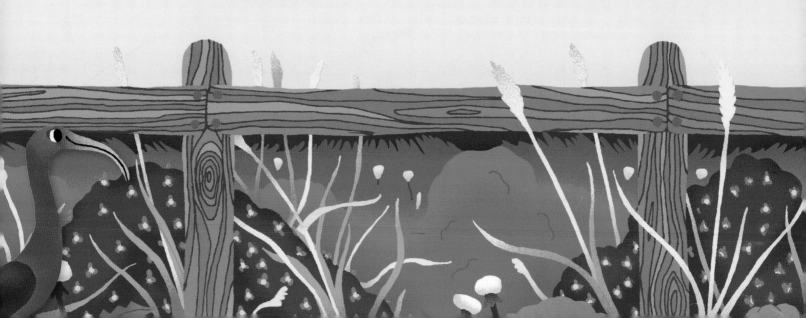

Introduction

Do you love nature and observing wildlife? Have you ever dreamed of roaming the globe to see the amazing birds that live in each habitat? Well get ready to travel with this book – from meadows and woodlands to deserts and mountains, you'll visit them all. All kinds of bird life are hidden in these pages, but it's harder than you think – birds are good at hiding and camouflaging themselves; they have to be, to avoid predators and to catch prey.

On each double-page spread you'll be taken to a different part of the world, given a picture and description of the birds you'll be looking for and left to search the landscape. So what are you waiting for? Grab your passport and start spotting our feathered friends! And while you're scanning the pages, can you also find the binoculars that an absent-minded bird spotter has left on each spread? If it all gets too much, the answers for birds and binoculars are at the back.

Enjoy!

Matt Sewell

Flowering meadow

Cirl buntings

In lush, flowering meadows across Europe, friendly cirl buntings love to frolic. Swaying in the long grass, nibbling on seeds and singing their hearts out from fence posts and spiky bushes, the sage green and buttery yellow bunting is a beauty of a spot.

Can you find **12** of the little yellow fellows hidden amongst the wild flowers?

Deep in the jungle

Ring-necked parakeet

"SQWAAARK" is the giveaway sound when there are parakeets around. This bird is so perfectly coloured to blend in with the jungle that it is funny to think that there are now thousands of these noisy emerald parrots living in London. They don't mind the cold or traffic; in fact they seem to thrive in those conditions.

Can you spot **10** ring-necked parakeets in the dense tropical undergrowth?

Wild sea cliff

Little auk

Up on the wild sea cliffs, hidden amongst guillemots and their puffin cousins, you can find the dovekie, otherwise known as the little auk. This is indeed the littlest of all the seagoing auks, and perhaps the cutest too. Which is no easy feat considering they are up against murrelets, puffins and crested auklets. They are as cute as a mermaid's rubber ducky!

Can you spot **23** little auks on and around this cliff, warming themselves in the sun after a day on the ocean?

Hot, dry desert

Desert cardinal

The desert cardinal also has the tongue-twisting name of Pyrrhuloxia. This amazing bird is fond of the scrubland and deserts of North America. Here, in their reddy-pink bandit masks, they zip about catching bugs and plucking cactus fruit all day long.

Can you spot **17** desert cardinals hidden in the mesquite thicket and saguaro cacti.

On the farm

Lapwing

It's hard to believe that something as shiny and eye-catching as the lapwing can be a master of disguise. But nesting in rough ground on farmland and pastures the green plover is camouflaged excellently amongst the grass and stone.

Can you hear them call 'peewit peewit' and spot all **16**?

Indian temple gardens

Indian roller

With its azure crown, sapphire wing vents and sky blue tail feathers the Indian roller is a truly handsome bird. He does love to show off his colours, and quite right too. But all birds need a place to rest undisturbed sometimes, so it's very handy that they can fit right in amongst the splendid palace gardens of India that they call home.

Can you find all **9** resting Indian rollers?

Oasis in the city

Goldfinch

Before the park opens its gates to the busy city folk, a charm of goldfinches are taking advantage of the peace and quiet and enjoying a game of hide and seek. Often found in large flocks the golden finches have fun and play together all year round, chiming like bells as they go.

Can you find **13** hidden in the park?

High in the Alps

Northern wheatear

If you're climbing the slopes of the Alps and keep seeing flashes of blue and white in front of you, it will most likely be the rump of the mountaineering wheatear disappearing into the distance. Lover of rocks and heather, this blue bird of the peaks is a fantastic spot when you can get close enough.

Can you spot **7** wheatears hidden amongst the mountain flowers and heather?

Into the woods

Willow tit

It may be possible that in any section of woodland across Europe, North America, Russia and parts of Asia you will find a willow tit or one of their many cousins. In fact tits and chickadees can be found in most of the northern hemisphere. Our willow tit here is one of the smaller and shyer ones. Their green tones blend in perfectly with the forest, keeping them secret and safe.

Can you find **14** willow tits as they search for their dinner?

In the city

Tree sparrow

In Europe the tree sparrow, with chestnut cap and big sideburns, is normally a woodland and countryside bird (as you can imagine by the name). In Asia, massive colonies of them have been lured by bright lights and fancy living, and have moved to the city. You will find whole flocks busily window shopping, begging for scraps and foraging the city trees for their usual seed and nut-based snacks.

Can you find **27** of these feathered-city-folk as they go about their day?

The sunny Serengeti

Glossy ibis

With its sickle-like beak, the ibis is a distinctive bird found all over the world. Here in the Serengeti is the glossy ibis with its deep red metallic coat and long hooked bill. The beak is perfect for picking insects from the water's edge that the flamingos have failed to spot from their lofty height.

Can you spot **22** glossy ibises amongst the 125 pink flamingos?

In the snowy pines

Siberian jay

Where the forest ends and the mountains begin is where you will find the hardy and rugged Siberian jay. Here in the snow-covered pines the jay hides his food in the ground, stored for especially cold days.

Can you find **5** Siberian jays sheltering from the snow and the fearsome goshawk?

Bedtime in the rainforest

Black baza

The black baza is a night hawk of South-east Asia and India. With his small frame (about as big as a blackbird) and glossy dark coat, he is perfectly designed to gather midnight feasts. This small bird of prey comes out at dusk to catch his favourite meal of bugs – yes, he eats the creepy crawlies that come out after dark in the hot, steamy rainforest!

Can you spot **15** of the hawks on this starry night in the jungle?

Answers

How did you do in the big bird spot? Did you find all of the feathered friends?
And how about the binoculars? Check your answers below.

The labels will also help you to identify the other wildlife on the pages.

Flowering meadow

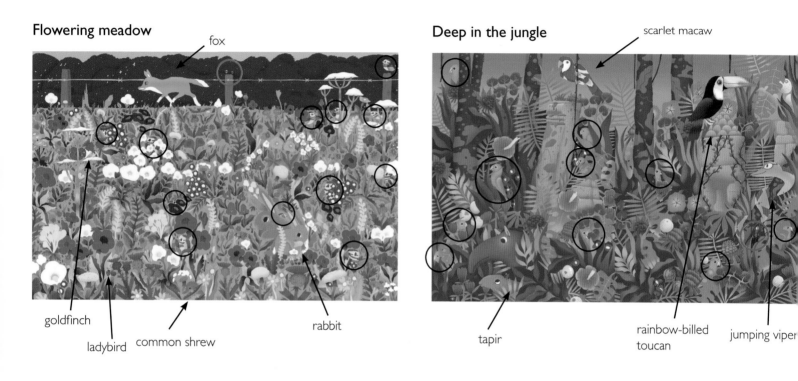

fox

goldfinch

ladybird

common shrew

rabbit

Deep in the jungle

scarlet macaw

tapir

rainbow-billed toucan

jumping viper

Wild sea cliff

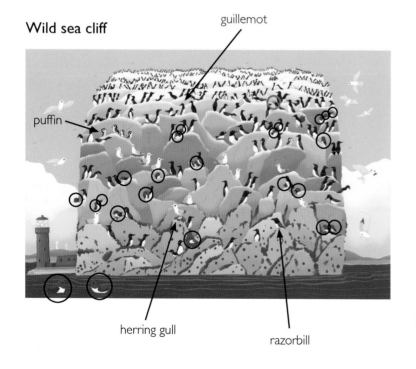

guillemot

puffin

herring gull

razorbill

Hot, dry desert

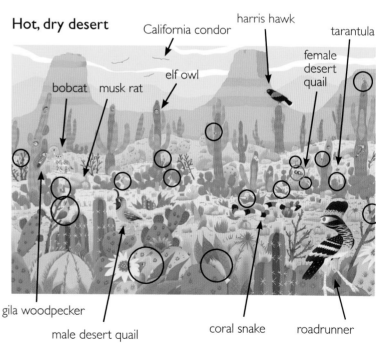

California condor

harris hawk

tarantula

bobcat

musk rat

elf owl

female desert quail

gila woodpecker

male desert quail

coral snake

roadrunner

On the farm

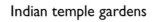

male kestrel

curlew

linnet

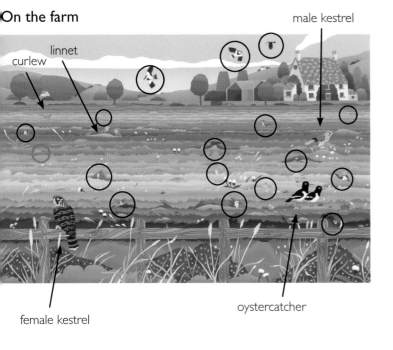

female kestrel

oystercatcher

Indian temple gardens

peacock

tiger

Oasis in the city

robin

wren

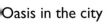

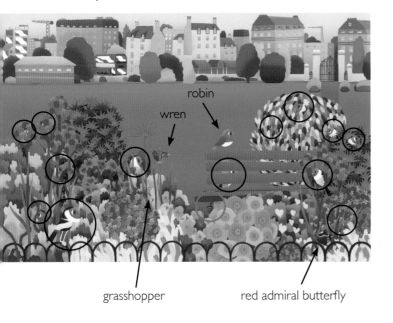

grasshopper

red admiral butterfly

High in the Alps

wallcreeper

black grouse

Into the woods

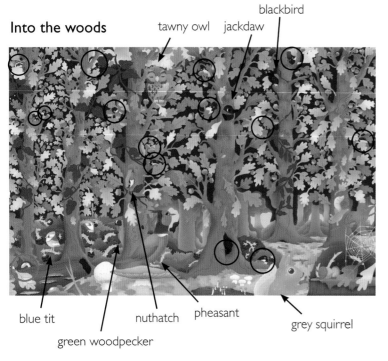

tawny owl
jackdaw
blackbird

blue tit
green woodpecker
nuthatch
pheasant
grey squirrel

In the city

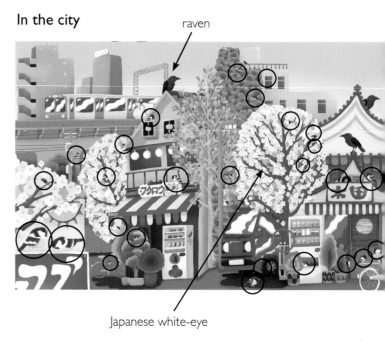

raven

Japanese white-eye

The sunny Serengeti

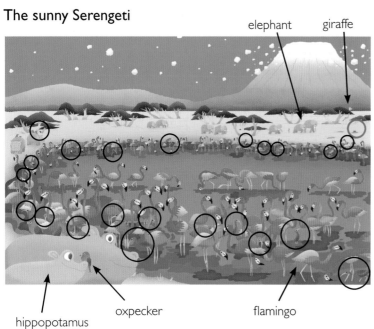

elephant
giraffe

hippopotamus
oxpecker
flamingo

In the snowy pines

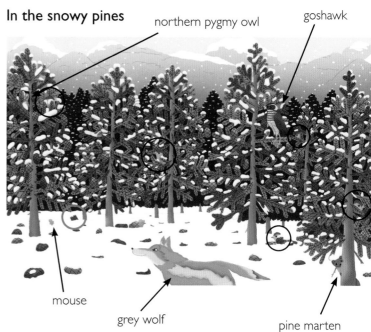

northern pygmy owl
goshawk

mouse
grey wolf
pine marten

Bedtime in the rainforest

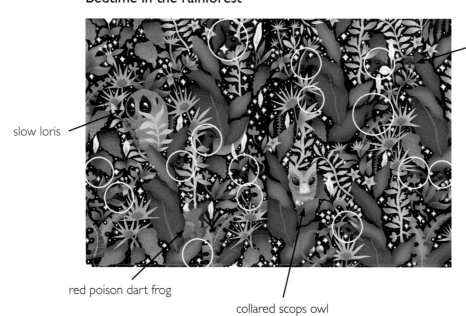

bumble bee bat

slow loris

red poison dart frog

collared scops owl

Keep looking for those
birds in real life too!
Make a record of
the ones you see.

Happy spotting!